W9-AVO-156

Spotlight on the 13 Colonies
Birth of a Nation

★ ★ ★ ★ ★ ★ ★ ★ ★ ★ ★ ★ ★

THE COLONY OF
NEW JERSEY

Maggie Misztal

PowerKiDS press™

NEW YORK

Published in 2016 by The Rosen Publishing Group, Inc.
29 East 21st Street, New York, NY 10010

Editor: Sarah Machajewski
Book Design: Andrea Davison-Bartolotta

Photo Credits: Cover MPI/Stringer/Getty Images; pp. 4 (inset), 17 Stock Montage/Getty Images; pp. 4–5 (main)
Keith Sherwood/Shutterstock.com; pp. 7, 9, 14–15 North Wind Picture Archive; pp. 10, 11, 16, 19 Courtesy
of Library of Congress; p. 12 (inset) Print Collector/Getty Images; pp. 12–13 (main) Andrew F. Kazmierski/
Shutterstock.com; p. 13 (inset) Courtesy of New Jersey State Archives/Department of State; p. 21 Courtesy of U.S.
Army Center of Military History; p. 22 VectorPic/Shutterstock.com.

Cataloging-in-Publication Data

Misztal, Maggie.
The colony of New Jersey / by Maggie Misztal.
p. cm. — (Spotlight on the 13 colonies: Birth of a nation)
Includes index.
ISBN 978-1-4994-0531-6 (pbk.)
ISBN 978-1-4994-0533-0 (6 pack)
ISBN 978-1-4994-0534-7 (library binding)
1. New Jersey — History — Colonial period, ca. 1600 - 1775 — Juvenile literature. 2. New Jersey — History —
1775 - 1865 — Juvenile literature. I. Title.
F137.M57 2016
974.9—d23

Manufactured in the United States of America

CPSIA Compliance Information: Batch #WS15PK: For further information contact Rosen Publishing, New York, New York at 1-800-237-9932.

Contents

Precolonial New Jersey

New Jersey is a mid-Atlantic state on the eastern coast of the United States. It's bordered by New York, Pennsylvania, Delaware, and the Atlantic Ocean. New Jersey is the fourth-smallest state, but its history is far from tiny.

Native Americans occupied the land that's now New Jersey long before Europeans arrived. The Lenni Lenape, also known as the Delaware, had little contact with whites before the seventeenth century.

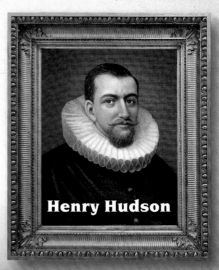

Henry Hudson

New Jersey

Hudson River

The first European to reach New Jersey was an Italian explorer named Giovanni da Verrazano in 1524. However, the land was not settled for another 85 years. In 1609, English explorer Henry Hudson and his crew sailed into Sandy Hook Bay. They were exploring on behalf of the Netherlands' Dutch East India Company.

Other Europeans began arriving in the area soon after Hudson's adventures there. Most of them were farmers. The Dutch founded the first **permanent** settlement in New Jersey in 1660. They named it Bergen; today it's known as Jersey City.

The Hudson River, which acts as the border between present-day New Jersey and New York, was named after Henry Hudson.

New York

The Dutch and the British

The Dutch began establishing settlements in North America in the early 1600s. They created the Dutch West India Company to oversee all colonization activity in North America. The first Dutch colonists arrived in present-day Manhattan in 1624. The Dutch named their claim "New Netherland," which later came to include settlements in present-day New Jersey.

Sweden had established a colony called New Sweden that lay partly in the southern part of present-day New Jersey. Settlers there had come from Sweden and other countries, such as Finland. The Dutch took control of New Sweden in 1655 and made it part of New Netherland.

Britain was interested in colonizing North America, too. It had claimed lands between Canada and Florida, and had established colonies in the New England and the Chesapeake Bay regions by the early 1600s. Britain and the Dutch fought over their land claims. In 1664, Britain took control of the land that's today New Jersey.

This map shows New Sweden, which lasted from 1638 to 1655. Swedish colonists left a unique historical **legacy**: log cabins. The oldest standing log cabin is located in Gibbstown, New Jersey.

Creating New Jersey

In 1664, King Charles II gave New Amsterdam to his brother, the duke of York. New Amsterdam was a Dutch settlement where New Netherland's colonial government was located. The area was renamed New York in the duke of York's honor.

In 1664, the duke of York split off a small piece of land between the Hudson and the Delaware Rivers. He gave it to Sir George Carteret and Lord John Berkeley. The colony was named after the Isle of Jersey in England, where Carteret was governor.

George Carteret and John Berkeley did much for the New Jersey colony's early days. Carteret's cousin, Philip Carteret, was appointed the colony's first governor. They founded major towns, including Elizabethtown and Newark. In 1664, the men issued a **document** called the Concessions and Agreement. It said New Jersey colonists would be considered free and were **guaranteed** religious freedom. It also called for the colony to have an elected body of **representatives** that could make laws.

Philip Carteret arrives in New Jersey.

East and West

Though the British were happy with their claims in New Jersey, the Dutch were not. They fought to get their land back and briefly reclaimed some of New Jersey in 1673. Britain gained the land back in 1674.

John Berkeley sold his claims to British Quakers in 1674. In 1676, New Jersey was divided into two **provinces**. The Quakers controlled West Jersey, which was formerly Berkeley's land. George Carteret controlled East Jersey until his death in 1680. Carteret's family sold East Jersey to the Quakers after he died. William Penn, a Quaker who founded the colony of Pennsylvania, was a big part of this purchase.

Quakers were members of a religious group called the Society of Friends. Their beliefs were different from those of many people in England. They wanted a place to practice their religion freely. The Jerseys became known as a place that offered political and religious freedom. It was attractive to Quakers, but people from many backgrounds settled in the Jersey colony.

Quaker meetinghouse, Princeton, NJ

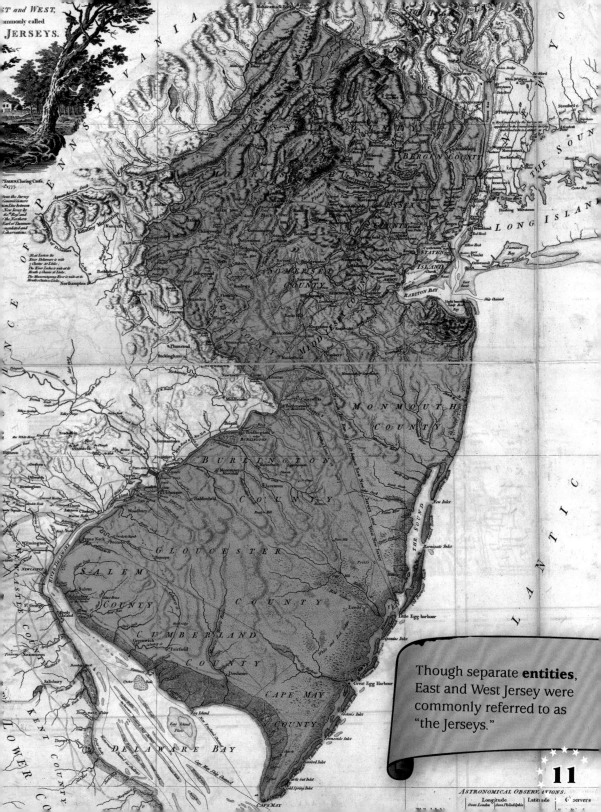

ST and WEST,
commonly called
JERSEYS.

Though separate **entities**, East and West Jersey were commonly referred to as "the Jerseys."

ASTRONOMICAL OBSERVATIONS.

Rebellious New Jersey

East and West Jersey remained divided until 1702, when Britain's Queen Anne joined them together. From then on, New Jersey was a royal colony governed by the British crown.

The British crown appointed royal governors for its colonial claims. New Jersey shared a governor with New York colony for a long time. In 1738, New Jersey finally got its own governor, Lewis Morris.

Queen Anne

Throughout New Jersey's colonial history, there had been problems between the government and colonists over collecting rent and taxes. Part of the problem was that the land had been owned by many different people. Colonists often didn't know who owned the land on which they lived. Land riots broke out in the 1740s between colonists and landowners over taxes. Some historians believe this **rebelliousness** was the first sign of the revolutionary spirit that would appear later during the colonies' fight for independence.

This **petition** asks the General Assembly of Burlington, New Jersey, to pardon the rioters in northern New Jersey. The author says the rioters now see their actions as illegal and wrong. The document asks for an "Act of Grace" for the rioters and to have the titles to the disputed lands tried fairly in front of an impartial judge.

Jersey Blues

In 1754, Britain once again entered into conflicts over land. Britain and France fought for control of land in North America that both countries wanted. France owned land in present-day Canada. It also owned land west of Britain's 13 colonies. Britain wanted this land so it could expand its territory west. This led to fighting, which we now call the French and Indian War.

New Jersey colony was far enough from the front lines that it didn't experience much of the war's action. However, in 1755, a series of Indian raids in northwest New Jersey caused colonists to form a **regiment** of 1,000 men, now known as the Jersey Blues. The Jersey Blues fought in many battles. Many men were captured at Fort Oswego in New York 1756. Many died during a battle at Lake George in New York in 1757. New Jersey soldiers fought against Indian attacks until 1758, when a truce with the Lenni Lenape ended the fighting between the two groups.

New Jersey soldiers helped the British win the French and Indian War.

Protesting Taxes

Britain won the war, but it was costly. Britain had to pay back money it had borrowed to pay for the war. It also needed money to keep British troops in the colonies to keep peace between colonists and Native Americans. Britain decided to raise money by taxing colonists.

The Stamp Act of 1765 required colonists to pay a tax on every piece of paper they bought. This angered New Jersey colonists. Governor William Franklin was so surprised by their anger and threats to **protest** that he didn't enforce the tax in the colony, despite his loyalty to Britain.

In June 1765, the Massachusetts Assembly invited leaders from the colonies to meet to discuss their issues with the Stamp

Stamp Act riot

Act. New Jersey sent Joseph Borden, Hendrick Fisher, and Robert Ogden to the meetings in New York City. The Stamp Act Congress, as it's now called, sent the king a letter explaining its disagreement with Britain's taxes. In 1766, Britain ended the Stamp Act.

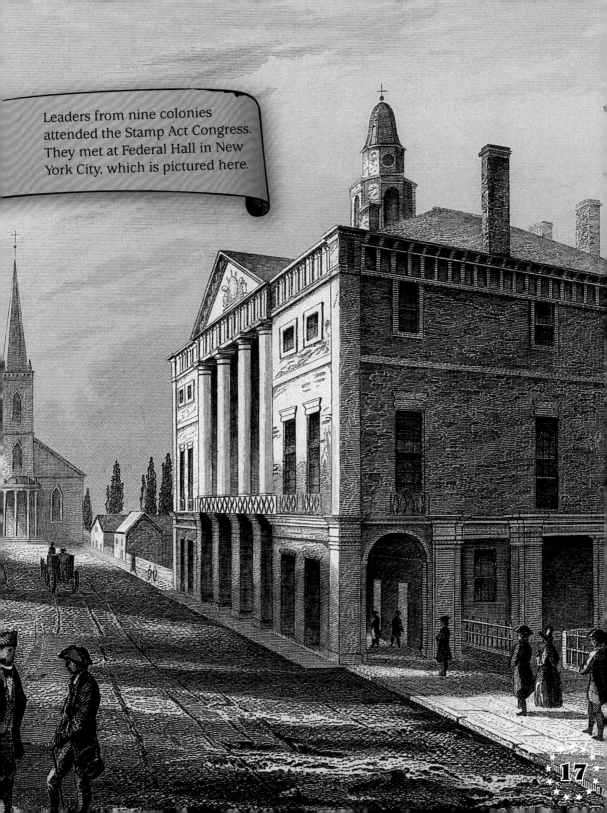

Leaders from nine colonies attended the Stamp Act Congress. They met at Federal Hall in New York City, which is pictured here.

Declaring Independence

Ending the Stamp Act didn't solve the problems between Britain and its colonies. In fact, they only got worse. In 1774, **delegates** from 12 of the 13 colonies met at Carpenter's Hall in Philadelphia. Stephen Crane, John de Hart, William Livingston, James Kinsey, and Richard Smith represented New Jersey. This series of meetings is now known as the First Continental Congress. The First Continental Congress sent a list of objections to Britain, and Britain sent more troops to the colonies.

The Revolutionary War began in April 1775, when fighting broke out at Lexington and Concord in Massachusetts. A few months later, colonial delegates returned to Philadelphia. The Second Continental Congress, as it's now called, voted whether or not to remain under British rule. On July 4, 1776, the American colonies declared their independence. Fifty-six delegates signed the Declaration of Independence. Five of them were from New Jersey: Abraham Clark, Francis Hopkinson, John Witherspoon, John Hart, and Richard Stockton.

The Second Continental Congress was responsible for establishing the Continental army. This illustration shows two soldiers marching during winter, which was often a tough season for the army.

"Crossroads of the Revolution"

Some **colony-states** greatly supported independence, but New Jersey was divided. About half its population remained loyal to the king. Even so, New Jersey was heavily involved in the fighting during the American Revolution. Almost 300 battles occurred on its soil, earning the colony-state the nickname "Crossroads of the Revolution."

Some of the war's most important battles were fought in New Jersey, especially the Battle of Trenton. On December 26, 1776, George Washington led the Continental army across the Delaware River from Pennsylvania into New Jersey. The troops landed and marched to the city of Trenton, where they launched a surprise attack on **Hessian** troops. The Continental army captured almost 900 enemy soldiers and much-needed supplies, such as guns and cannons.

A week later, Washington and his troops returned to New Jersey and won the Battle of Princeton. The Battles of Trenton and Princeton were important victories. They helped a weakened army feel strong and **confident** that it could take on the British.

This image shows the Continental army fighting Hessian troops during the Battle of Trenton.

The Third State

The Revolutionary War ended in 1783. The new United States first followed a set of laws called the Articles of Confederation. These laws weren't very successful, so representatives met in 1787 to discuss them. David Brearly, Jonathan Dayton, William C. Houston, William Livingston, and William Paterson represented New Jersey.

The representatives couldn't figure out a way to make the Articles of Confederation work. They ended up writing a new set of laws, called the Constitution. The Constitution says every state should have equal representation in one part of Congress—the Senate. This idea came from William Paterson, who didn't want tiny New Jersey to have less representation than larger states. These meetings, which occurred in Philadelphia, are now known as the Constitutional Convention.

In order for the Constitution to pass, it needed to be ratified, or accepted, by at least nine states. New Jersey ratified the Constitution on December 18, 1787, and became the third state in the United States of America.

Glossary

colony-state: A term for the American colonies when they were no longer colonies under Britain's rule, but not yet free and independent states.

confident: Sure of oneself.

delegate: A person sent to a meeting or convention to represent others.

document: A piece of written matter that provides information or that serves as an official record.

entity: Something with independent existence.

guarantee: To make sure.

Hessian: A German soldier paid to fight for the British during the American Revolution.

legacy: Something handed down over generations.

permanent: Made to last forever.

petition: A formal written request.

protest: To go against.

province: A division of a country.

rebelliousness: The quality of wanting to disobey authority.

regiment: A unit of an army.

representative: Someone who is chosen to act or speak for other people.

Index

Primary Source List

Page 10. Stony Brook Quaker Meetinghouse. Built by the Religious Society of Friends of the settlement of Stony Brook. Stone and timber. Constructed in 1724 and rebuilt in 1760. Now located in Princeton, NJ.

Page 11. *The Province of New Jersey, Divided into East and West, commonly called the Jerseys.* Created by William Faden after surveys by Bernard Ratzer and Gerard Banker. Hand-colored engraving. Included in Faden's *The North American Atlas*, published in 1777 in London, United Kingdom. Now kept at the Library of Congress Geography and Map Division, Washington, D.C.

Page 13. Petition for forgiveness for New Jersey land rioters. Ink on paper. Created in the eighteenth century. Now kept at the New Jersey State Archives, Department of State, in Trenton, NJ.

Websites

Due to the changing nature of Internet links, PowerKids Press has developed an online list of websites related to the subject of this book. This site is updated regularly. Please use this link to access the list: www.powerkidslinks.com/s13c/jers